Where Animals Live

The World of Swans

Text by Jennifer Coldrey

Photographs by
Oxford Scientific Films

Gareth Stevens Publishing
Milwaukee

Where Swans Live

Swans are water birds. They like open stretches of calm water. You can find swans on ponds, lakes, and slow-moving rivers. Many swans live in salt water, too.

In the winter, many swans *migrate* to waters on the coast. There, the water may be choppy and cold, but it doesn't freeze over.

The best kind of lake has lots of plants and small *aquatic* animals to eat. Plants also provide nesting material and shelter.

A lake with gently sloping sides makes it easier for the swans to climb in and out of the water.

The Mute Swan

Mute Swans are well-known. They are tame and swim gracefully on lakes in cities and in the country. Mute Swans make some noise, but they are usually quiet. That is why they are called Mute Swans.

Their original home is Europe and Asia. But now they also live in North America, Australia, the Soviet Union, and South Africa.

The Mute Swan is a large bird with big wings. The beak is orange-red and has a black nail at the tip. The beak also has a black knob at the base, near the nostrils.

Mute Swans have very long necks with thick feathers. They also have large black, webbed feet.

Other White Swans ⬆

There are four other kinds of large white swans. All of them, like the Whooper Swan, live far north. Whooper Swans have straight necks and have a loud whooping call.

Bewick's Swans are like small Whooper Swans. Their call is a softer, more musical call. ⬇

↑

The Whistling Swan lives in Canada and the northern U.S. It has a high whistling call. Like the Whooper and Bewick's Swans, it migrates long distances — over a thousand miles — for the winter.

The Trumpeter Swan is the largest of the swans. It is rare and lives only in Alaska and northern Canada. Trumpeter Swans do not migrate south for the winter.

↓

Swans from the Southern Hemisphere

Not all swans are white. These Black Swans live in Australia and New Zealand. Black Swans are about as big as Mute Swans. Each wing has a white band along the back edge. Otherwise, its *plumage* is all black.

Black Swans live in very large groups — sometimes as many as 50,000 in one flock!

↑

The Black-necked and Coscoroba Swans live in
South America. The Black-necked Swan has pink
legs and feet. Its call is weak and sounds like a
toy trumpet!

The Coscoroba Swan also has pink legs and feet.
It is small and has white plumage with black tips
on the wings. It looks more like a goose than a
swan.

↓

The Swan's Body

Swans have large boat-shaped bodies. This streamlined shape helps them move through the water. Like paddles, their feet help swans push themselves through the water.

Swans use their long necks to find food underwater. Sometimes they tip their bodies forward. This is called "upending."

The feathers of swans keep them warm and dry. Swans keep their feathers waterproof by smearing them with oil from a special *gland* near the tail. The swan rubs its beak on the gland and combs it through each feather. This is called *preening*.

Once a year swans lose their feathers and grow a new set. This is called *molting*.

Movement on Land and in the Air

Swans are clumsy on land. Their broad webbed feet help them walk on mud and ice. But they can only waddle along slowly on land.

Swans are graceful fliers, however. They have big, strong wings that make powerful wingbeats. Swans fly with their necks outstretched and with their legs tucked underneath. Also, they use their tails to help them steer.

Swans are quite heavy, so they have trouble taking off and landing. When swans come in for a landing, they use their big feet to help them stop.

Swans often fly in a V or in a diagonal line. Some migrate very long distances — up to 1000 miles. They can also fly very fast — up to 50 miles per hour, and up to 70 miles per hour with the wind behind them! In clear weather, they may fly as high as 5000 feet. When the weather is bad, they stay closer to the ground.

Migrating swans travel mainly at night. During the day, they stop to feed and rest.

Food and Feeding

Swans mainly eat water plants. They use their flat bill to scoop up food from the mud or water. Swans sometimes eat small animals, too, such as insects, tadpoles, snails, and tiny fish.

Swans can also use their long necks to find food at the bottom of a pond.

Because they don't have teeth, swans swallow gritty pieces of stone that help grind up the food. This grit is stored in a special part of the stomach called the *gizzard.*

On the side of the swan's bill are little fringes.
These fringes catch the food and strain out the
mud and water.

15

Courtship and Mating

Swans do not breed until they are three to four years old.

Male swans will fight to protect their *territory* when they find a mate. These two males are fighting to claim a territory.

Males often ruffle up their feathers to attract a female. Here, a male Mute Swan, called a *cob,* is on the right. The female, called a *pen,* is on the left.

Before mating, the cob and pen go through a special courtship dance. They face each other and move their heads from side to side. Sometimes they rub their necks against each other, make "kissing" movements, and dip their bodies into the water. Finally, the male *fertilizes* the eggs inside the female's body.

The male and female swans usually stay together for life once they have started a family.

Nesting and Laying Eggs

Swans build their nests close to water in spring or early summer. A small island is a good place to build a nest because it is surrounded by water, away from land *predators*. Many swans come back to nest in the same place year after year.

Most swans nest in pairs. The cob chooses the spot. He then stays close to guard the nest. ➡

The pen lays one egg every other day until there is a *clutch* of five to eight eggs. She keeps them warm, or *incubates* them, by fluffing her feathers and sitting on the eggs.

←

The nest is very big, sometimes as much as 9 to 12 feet across and 3 feet deep! Its size keeps the baby swans safe from the water and from enemies in the lake.

The Young Swans ↑

It takes five weeks for the swan eggs to hatch.
The young swans, called *cygnets,* are born with
their eyes open. When they dry off, they become
bundles of fluffy down.

The cygnets break out of the eggs with a special
nail at the end of their beaks. This nail is very
sharp and is called an egg-tooth. It drops off a
few days after the cygnets hatch.

The young swans stay close to their mother for
warmth and protection.

Some swans, like this Mute Swan, carry their babies on their backs.

Baby swans know how to swim as soon as they are hatched. When they are only a day or two old, they follow their parents. Soon, they learn to find food for themselves.

Growing Up

As the cygnets get older, greyish brown feathers replace the down. The cygnets above are just over one month old. The Mute Swan cygnet on the right is about six months old. It still has a lot of greyish brown feathers.

The time when a young bird first flies is called *fledging*. Swans from the far north must be ready to fly south after a very short summer. They fledge in only two or three months. Other swans may take six months to fledge.

Swans are born in the summer and spend their first winter with their parents. Swans that migrate must go many days without food. They prepare for this by putting on lots of weight.

After their first winter, young swans usually leave their parents. Often the adults are eager to start a new family, and they drive the young swans away. Then, until they are ready to breed, young swans stay together in large flocks.

Enemies and Other Dangers

Swans are large, strong birds. They are able to defend themselves from attack. In fact, their hissing, snorting, flapping wings, and ruffled neck feathers are enough simply to scare away most enemies!

This Mute Swan is angry. It has raised its wings and is moving quickly across the water to protect its nest.

More than half of all chicks die before the end of their first winter. Those that survive can live to be 15 years old. Young swans suffer from the dangers of cold, hunger, and disease. Swans also often fly into buildings and overhead wires, or have other accidents in the air.

But the main enemies of swans attack swan eggs and young. These animals include foxes, wolves, dogs, coyotes, otters, and gulls. Sometimes large fish, like this pike, attack young swans swimming on the lake.

Humans as Enemies

Humans are among the worst enemies of swans. In the past, people hunted swans for food and collected their down for quilts and pillows. In the 19th Century, the Mute Swan was killed off in some parts of Europe, and the Trumpeter Swan nearly became *extinct* in North America. Today, it is illegal to shoot swans. Also, special laws protect most swans in their *habitats.*

People also harm swans by destroying or disturbing their habitats. When water is *polluted* by oil, fuel, *pesticides,* or other poisons, swans can be poisoned, too.

Fishermen can hurt swans by leaving fishing lines and hooks behind. Also, swans can get lead poisoning by swallowing the lead weights left by fishermen. The middle cygnet in the picture below is suffering from lead poisoning. You can tell because it cannot hold its neck up straight.

Friends and Neighbors

Geese, ducks, and other water birds often share the lake with swans. In winter, large numbers of birds may gather on the water.

Many water birds visit the lake only to find food. Some, like herons, will eat baby birds, and they can be a threat to swans with young cygnets.

Swans usually attack only when they are threatened by a dangerous enemy. But they will attack water birds and other animals that come too close to their territories and young.

Many water birds, including Canada Geese, nest around the edges of a lake. This Great Crested Grebe builds a nest like a floating platform. The nest is attached to reeds.

Other animals, such as otters, muskrats, and beavers, share the lake with swans. This American Beaver lives in Canada and the northern U.S. It is a neighbor of both the Trumpeter and Whistling Swans.

Life on the Lake

Swans are mainly plant-eaters. Many other birds feed on plants, too. But as this diagram shows, each kind of bird finds food in a different way. Some feed on different plants, and some feed in different parts of the lake. For example, when swans upend, they can feed in deeper water than geese. So there is competition for food, but there is usually enough for all.

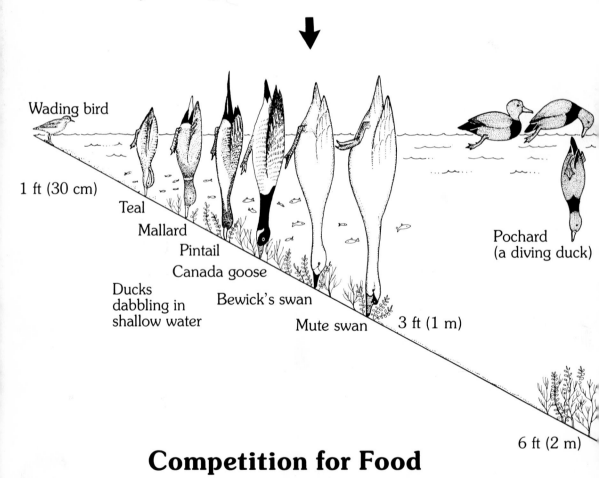

Competition for Food

Swans need plenty of food, shelter, and shallow stretches of water. They also need clean water and peace and quiet. That is why this clean, peaceful lake makes a perfect home for swans. That is also why we must protect the wild places where swans live. If we are to enjoy seeing these beautiful birds on our lakes, we must look after their homes.

Index and New Words About Swans

These new words about swans appear in the text on the pages shown after each definition. Each new word first appears in the text in *italics*, just as it appears here.

Reading level analysis: SPACHE 2.8, FRY 2, FLESCH 93 (very easy), RAYGOR 3, FOG 4, SMOG 3

Library of Congress Cataloging-in-Publication Data

Coldrey, Jennifer.
The world of swans.
(Where animals live)
Summary: Describes, in simple text and photographs, the lives of swans in their natural habitat explaining how they feed, defend themselves, and breed.
1. Swans -- Juvenile literature. [1. Swans] I. Oxford Scientific Films. II. Title. III. Series.
QL696.A52C653 1986   598.4'1   86-5721

ISBN 1-55532-095-3

ISBN 1-55532-070-8 (lib. bdg.)

North American edition first published in 1987 by
Gareth Stevens, Inc.
7221 West Green Tree Road   Milwaukee, Wisconsin 53223, USA
US edition, this format, copyright © 1987 by Belitha Press Ltd.
Text copyright © 1987 by Gareth Stevens, Inc.

First conceived, designed, and produced by Belitha Press Ltd., London, as **The Swan on the Lake**, with an original text copyright by Oxford Scientific Films. Format copyright by Belitha Press Ltd.
Typeset by Ries Graphics ltd., Milwaukee.
Printed in the United States of America.
Series Editor: Mark J. Sachner.
Art Director: Treld Bicknell.
Design: Naomi Games. Cover Design: Gary Moseley.
Scientific Consultants: Gwynne Vevers and David Saintsing.

The publishers wish to thank the following for permission to reproduce copyright material: **Oxford Scientific Films Ltd.** for pp. 4, 5, 8, 24, and 31 (photographer G.I Bernard); p. 22 and title page (photographer Alastair Shay); pp. 2, 12, and back cover (photographer David Cayless); pp. 3, 10, 15 above, 19, 25 below, 26, and 28 (photographer David Thompson); p. 6 both (photographer L.B. Blossom); pp. 7 above and 9 below (photographer Peter O'Toole); p. 7 below (photographer Margot Conte); p. 8 (photographer J.A.L. Cooke); p. 9 above (photographer H.W. Price); pp. 11, 14, 15 below, and 21 below (photographers David and Sue Cayless); p. 13 (photographer Barry Walker); pp. 16 and 21 above (photographer Mike Birkhead); p. 17 (photographer Martyn Chillmaid); pp. 20 and 23 (photographer Richard Packwood); pp. 25 above and 27 and front cover (photographer C.M. Perrins); p. 29 above (photographer D.J. Saunders); p. 29 below (photographer Harry Engels).